DIRTBAG INNOVATIONS

DIRTBAG INNOVATIONS

FIELD GUIDE TO TRAVELING AS CHEAP AS POSSIBLE

4 Years
35 States
14,000 Dollars
and a Bus

FIELD GUIDE TO TRAVELING
AS CHEAP AS POSSIBLE

Editing Services provided by Stacey Smekofske
www.editsbystacey.com

Formatting by TeaBerryCreative.com

ISBN: Print: 979-8-9862853-0-6
eBook 979-8-9862853-1-3

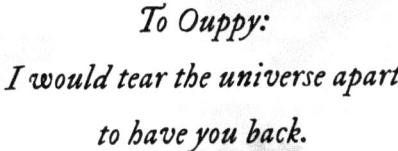

To Ouppy:
I would tear the universe apart
to have you back.

Find your truth and live it.

—ANTHONY

CONTENTS

INTRODUCTION

IN 2012, I BOUGHT A BUS for $1,700 to move to the west coast. Four years later, I found myself living out of that bus with my fabrication tools and my pup. A lot happened from 2013 to 2016, but the key takeaways were my passion for minimalist living and rock climbing.

Rock climbing became my world, leading to a life at Smith Rock for an entire summer. The following winter, the house I was renting went up for sale. After three months of looking for a new house, I could not find a place for me the pup and my fab shop. I decided to move into my bus out of necessity.

At the time, climbing had become such a driving force in my life that I decided to take a month-long climbing trip in the bus. Four years later, I had cashed in both my 401Ks, had about 700 dollars to my name, had lived and climbed in 35 states, had driven cross country five times, and had lived a lifetime of dreams. All told, the entire adventure only cost $15,700.

Tiny living was not mainstream in that day. There was no Instagram page on that way of life; there was no place to go for resources. It was all trial and error. Now there are about a million #vanlife, #tinyliving, and #schoolie pages out there. They all sell the dream of life on the road. They tell you how wonderful tiny living is, inspiring the population to give up the "white picket fence" programming and take our lives back. But that's just a bunch of pictures and cute quotes about how beautiful it is to wake up and see the mountains out the back door. In reality, the vanlife movement is relatively new. It is not quite old enough for a collection of data points, for resourcing.

In the following pages I will share all the tips and tricks I learned along the way about money, gas, food, tiny living, and travel. It is my hope that you will be able to use this guide to help you live your life full of adventure and purpose, skipping the big Oh-Fuck struggles and mistakes. My four years of trial and error on the road and six years of bus life can be those data points to help you along the way.

WANDERLUST

WHEN I FIRST GOT ON THE ROAD, I had all these plans of things I wanted to do and places I wanted to go. I kept trying to make the things happen; I wanted to have all the *Epics*. Boy did I ever have some Epics that first couple of months. I was always in a rush to get to the next place and do the next thing. However, they weren't quality Epics. They were the everything-just-went-horribly-wrong-and-now-I-can't-enjoy-what-I'm-doing Epics. There were things I missed and people I didn't meet because I was so focused on the itinerary. It took a while for me to learn that the universe is a much stronger force than I am and to not fight it.

Slow down and see the opportunities in front of you.

I learned very quickly that I'm a pendulum with a wide swing. I'm always at one end or the other, and I find it so hard to live in the middle. I wandered around for a couple of months with no plan and went where the universe directed me. After a year on the road, I figured out how to have a loose itinerary and flow *with* the universe. I learned how to plan *with* the universe. That's when it all kind of clicked for me. I learned to know all the things I want to see, do, and experience, but I understood that they might not happen in an orderly fashion. That was the key for me. I keep a mental list of what I want, and I get to it when the universe brings me within arm's reach of it.

Be open to all opportunities that present themselves and talk to everyone.

If you've met me, this will come as an extreme shock. I have severe social anxiety and am, by default, very shy and self-conscience. Those first three months on the road were super lonely for me. In fact, the only human interaction I had was when I would stop to fill up with diesel, and then only if I had to pay inside.

Ouppy is an amazing companion. When we hit the road, he was only nine and had spent almost his entire life growing up on the family farm. The transition to roaming around the country was very easy for him. At first, I didn't notice how lonely I had become, because we spent all our time in national forests climbing and hiking away from society. Ouppy has been my ESA since he was about two years old, and he does a damn good job of minimizing my social anxiety and recognizing my emotional state.

The first time we went to a coffee shop to do internet things was when I really noticed how deprived of human connection I was. I wasn't the type to just randomly talk to someone. There had to be a reason to talk, or I wouldn't, no matter how much I wanted to. It was just too overwhelming. Luckily Ouppy has the most inviting eyes of any creature, and just about everyone who meets him wants to pet him. It made it easier to start conversations. Ouppy was the focus and took the pressure off me. Once I started sharing what I was doing, people's eyes would light up and the questions would flood in. More importantly, the help and advice would also come in. I would hear, "Oh, you absolutely have to see this while you're here," or "Make sure to not miss this if you're heading that way," but the most important statements were the "Watch out for this in that place," or "I know someone you should meet."

The connections you will make from these interactions could last a lifetime and the help you can receive could be priceless.

It's totally the degrees of separation game. Someone you meet in Indiana might know a person in Colorado that you don't know you need in your life yet. They will have that epic spot to park your rig. More importantly they might know that one person that can drive two hours into the desert with their mobile mechanic setup and save you and your rig. They might just do it for free because you change someone's life in Georgia that means the world to them.

I cannot express how important it is to talk to everyone. Don't just *shoot the shit* with everyone you pass; instead, take interest and invest in that human connection. Invest in every gas station attendant, every barista, every grocery store clerk, everyone you stand in line with.

Get off your phone
and make connections.
The rewards are limitless.

I first went to Moab in 2015, after climbing
with a group of guys in their late 40s who had
just flown in from NY for a climbing trip. At the
time, I was 29 and had met them at the parking site
for crag in Boulder. I had driven out there in the
morning, and they were the first climbers to show
up. They were a group of 5, so I asked if they wanted
to even out the numbers so everyone had a part-
ner. They let me join and ended up inviting me to
rope gun for them the entire week of their trip. We
met at the same place every morning for breakfast,
never letting me pay. They always brought lunch
for us and would take me for drinks and food at the
end of the night. On the last night, they asked if I
had ever been to Moab. I had not. They told me I
had to go; the place was pure magic. So, on a whim,
I went there, and rope soloed from 7:00 a.m. to
7:00 p.m. They were right; Moab won my heart.
It was the most meaningful place I had ever been.

Three years later Moab called to me again, so I posted in the local Acro page looking for a place to park my bus. Famous slackliner, Michelle Griffin, reached out to the Acro community in Portland to vet me. She offered a place for me to stay behind her house. I stayed for two weeks, and I cannot express the gratitude I have for her and my time in Moab. All the local dirtbags, river rats, slackliners, and outdoor enthusiasts heard I was staying at her place, and they took me on so many great adventures.

Currently the price of a "Cataract Canyon Whitewater Rafting experience" starts at the rate of $625 per person. Holy shit! It's a strict, *by the book, don't stray from the path* guided rafting tour. It's kind of like a guided horse ride. Here's your horse, there's the trail, follow the horse in front of you. Do not trot; do not get off trail and remember to enjoy yourself. It's the experience without the actual experience. You never actually get to participate, and you're just along for the ride.

I met two rafting guides while in Moab. Both loved rafting, but like most of us, they hated doing it for work. Guiding was not enjoyable to them, because it was so controlled that it never allowed for a real connection with the environment or the participants. All they wanted to do on their days off was ride on the river and have the real moments, sharing their love for the river with humans that could appreciate it. I went whitewater rafting six times in the two weeks I was there. That's $3750 worth of experience that I never had to pay for. All they ever asked for in return was love, smiles, good conversation, and respect for the river. Oh, and to help inflate and deflate the rafts.

Michelle was talking with a local, Helena, about the dirtbag climber that lived in a bus staying in her back yard. Helena had a Volkswagen Westphalia and they started talking about my build out. Now if you remember it was a 20-foot Thomas built dog nose. In 2016 I had moved my shop and me into it. To put it into perspective, it was a six-window bus; the shop took up four windows. The dog and I lived in the front two window spaces. The bed was above the windows with the kitchen underneath, and my living space was outside the bus, in nature.

When they heard that I was a metal fabricator with a mobile fab shop, they quickly asked if I could fix the pop top, which had ripped off in a sudden windstorm. I drove out, had a look at it and immediately started working on it. That's when I realized what I wanted the rest of my life to be.

I woke up this morning to this text message conversation with Michelle in Moab.

MICHELLE: Babe! You in Portland these days?

ME: Sure am

MICHELLE: Would love to see you.

ME: Coffee this morning?

MICHELLE: I've gotta work my muggle job.

But in general yes... got a reco for a place I CAN GO TO WORK?

Rn I'm in Vancouver so I have to take an Uber somewhere

ME: I'll snatch you and take you to my fave spot to work.

I actually have some work to do this morning also.

Did you bring a harness

MICHELLE: Haha i did actually, but no shoes

ME: We can make that work

Grab it

I've written the last four paragraphs of this guide, sitting across from this amazing human at my favorite coffee shop (Cathedral Coffee) in the city I currently call home and run my business out of. I am living the life I imagined in 2018 all because I went to the parking spot for a crag in Boulder.

Make every connection you can.

Since the day we start school, pretty much till the day we die, we end up standing in lines. When we were younger, we passed the time in line by talking to whoever was in front or behind us. Somewhere along the line, we stopped interacting with the other humans in line. Now it's like we are in line on another dimension from those around us. My favorite thing to do is make eye contact and say, "Do you have the mental and emotional space to get to know a complete stranger while we wait in line?" Very rarely does this fail to start a conversation.

Through all the talking I did with everyone around me, I ended up being put in touch with a

farm in Elizabethtown, Kentucky that needed a
farm hand. I talked to someone about how I had
grown up on a draft horse farm. That person told
someone about the guy they met at the coffee shop
that lived out of a school bus, wore a cowboy hat,
and grew up on a horse farm. That person knew
a farm that was looking for a hand and might be
willing to let me live on-site. That's how I spent
three months living at a boarding stable in Elizabethtown from summer to the start of fall. That
allowed to spend four days camping and climbing
in Red River Gorge.

 The deal we worked out was I would get a work
vehicle (the first Geo Tracker I ever drove) and
unlimited fuel to run errands and climb. I had my

own small corner in the back forty of the farm where I could park the bus and have a private quiet home space. I had autonomy over my work hours, so much as I kept up on upkeep of the farm. I would always be available for emergency situations. The owner of the farm was a former Ranger Training Superior for the US Army. I started making local climbing friends and having them to the farm for bonfires and the like; Thursdays turned into "Tactical Knot Tying Thursdays." This is how I learned the Bowline knot and started using it exclusively for lead climbing. It took about a month of living on the farm to become close with everyone that worked there.

CLIMBING

OVER THE FOUR YEARS I spent on the road, I lived and climbed in 35 different states. I have what I call "forever homes" in Kentucky, Illinois, Wisconsin, Minnesota, California, Missouri, Oregon, Washington, Utah, Idaho, and New Mexico. It is all because of climbing and the friends I made through climbing. I'M GOOD AT IT. I don't mean I'm proficient or I can do it without thinking. I mean I live it.

I spent six hours a day almost every day for a year straight at Planet Granite. I would watch top-tier climbers climb routes. I learned how they worked that route, and I observed all their movements. I then trained my body until my body understood why you lean this way and moved that foot before shifting the other way and moving that hand. I made it my goal to go from no climbing experience to leading a 12a climb in a year. I was so dedicated to this goal that I overdid it, and I had an injury that put me in recovery from month nine to eleven. By week two of month eleven, I recovered to my pre-injury condition. By this time, all the employees and everyone that climbed in the evening at Planet Granite knew how close I was to my goal. I would start with a proper warm up and then attempt one 12a a night. I then spend the rest of the night working all the parts I struggled with until I could run through them with ease.

The climbing community is one of the most supportive groups I've ever belonged to. The gym would go dead silent when I started flaking my rope at a 12a, so it felt like it was just my belayer and me in the gym. I put my shoes on, chalked up, and got to it. I flew up the start of the route with ease, saw the crux took a sec to shake out. My belayer called up, "You got this Anthony. Move through it. GO!" My body flexed, did as it was a commanded. I did the moves like I was on auto pilot. I was completely gassed the next three clips, but somehow not pumped, and I made it to the top. As soon as

I clipped the last clip of the anchor, I screamed, "Fuck yes!" and took a victory whip. The entire staff yelled their support and everyone there congratulated me when I was on ground.

That next summer, I spent all my free time at Smith Rock. But the rest of that winter, I spent time preparing for outdoor climbing. I did a lot of research on rescue and wilderness aid training. I bought all the gear and practiced everything I had researched until it was engrained in my head. I learned the proper way to use all the gear I had, and I learned all the things that could go wrong.

It was an amazing summer of climbing with my best friend, Adam. We would get there on a Thursday, climb together until Saturday (when the rest of our friends could make it out), and then spent the weekends guiding and teaching them to properly outdoor climb. I ended up taking all this skill and knowledge on the road and helping gym climbers get outside safely.

Sounds like quite an experience, right? I was living out of a school bus, traveling across the country, climbing, backpacking, and being in nature all the time! It was an epic experience. And everyone I talked to about it would always say how they wished they could just take off and live that life. My suggestion was always, "Just do it. The longer you wait, the harder it will get." Which was always met with, "I wish."

This was usually my in. The wish was the way to get somewhere without it costing me anything. I offered a trade, "When are you free next? I'll take you climbing. You bring all the food and drive, and I'll take care of everything else." I went on so many mini-trips this way and spent little to no money doing it. One time, I went from Lexington, Kentucky, all the way to Virginia to hike fifty miles on the Appalachian Trail for four days, and it only cost me $30.

Be amazing at something!

Be able to offer something that is not readily obtainable to the regular citizen.

Use your knowledge as currency.

The price of hiring a rock climbing guide for a day is about $380 dollars a day. The amount of bartering and negotiating I did on the road was astounding. The skills I learned from all of this has translated so well to what I do now. I'm always finding or making deals on vehicles that I build out or things I need for builds. I never stop having epic experiences.

Be Prepared: Prepare. Prepare For Everything.

Getting caught with your pants at your ankles, will drain the bank. It's those need-it-now moments that can set you back a lot. Take the time and think about your intentions while on the road. Where do you plan on going? what do you plan on doing? Who do you plan on seeing? What might be the circumstances of these parts? Could one destination lead you four miles down a gravel road that very sneakily turns from two lane to one where you eventually come around a blind corner to an 8% grade that doesn't allow for backing out. Now suddenly, you're in a canyon on a one-way road that has a locked gate at the end. A tow out of here is going to cost a small fortune. It happened to me, luckily my wheelbase was short enough to make a 30-point turn and get turned around. Have a spare tire, air compressor, patch kit, chains, extra filters, and extra fluids.

Having basic mechanical skills and engine diagnostic knowledge can usually save a trip and $300 at a shop. Prepare for all those Oh-Fuck moments.

WHAT IS ESSENTIAL?

LET'S START WITH YOU, and by you, I mean ME. The entire time I was on the road, I never bought anything new. Everything was used, and I never paid the marked price. Used-goods stores are usually willing to make deals to sell product, so it never hurts to make an offer on an item. If you don't need the item immediately, there is always time to find it at the lowest possible price. This requires a lot of foresight and planning for failure. Knowing that an item will only last a few more months and starting your search early will allow for an inexpensive find.

Make a very strict distinction between necessity and extra.

You can live without the extra things, which means you are going to have to get used to "being uncomfortable." Then you will find yourself altering your view of "comfortable" to only consuming and using what you need to survive.

I completely stopped using shampoo, soap, deodorant, underwear, socks, and shoes. Underwear, socks, deodorant, and shoes are all consumables that cost money. I changed my diet to only replace calories I lost throughout the day. I never stopped *showering*. In fact, my washing increased.

I was bathing in a body of water twice if not three times a day. There's always a stream or creek nearby.

My essentials included:

- 2 pairs of pants
- 2 pairs of shorts
- 2 short sleeved shirts
- 2 long sleeved shirts
- An entire base layer
- Jacket
- Foot protectors for winter and going in stores

I lived in shorts during the summer and barely ever wore a shirt. I would typically wear the same clothes for about a week, depending on my activity level. Most of the time, I was out in the woods by myself or with other outdoor enthusiasts, thus removing the concern of the soiled/stinking factor. Because I was so rarely in society where there is a strong demand for observing societal norms, I would designate one outfit as my *dress up* attire, and I could typically go about a month or so before needing to clean them.

> Determine and eliminate the non-essentials that wear out and must be replaced, eating up your valuable savings.

WASH UP

WASHING THE ESSENTIAL consisted of a river rinse every night before bed, allowing for a much longer intervals between actual washings.

Washing Clothes

Washing and drying an average load of laundry at a laundromat can range anywhere from $4 to $12 with the national average coming in at $6.20 a load, plus the cost of detergent.

We live in a world of immediate access, but it comes at a cost.

That cost is of course your money, and inevitably that can translate to your experiences. As we know, everything costs money. Yes, national forests are free, but fuel to get there isn't. Doing things like air drying clothes and using river water to wash yourself and your things, can mitigate those costs.

Cleaning House

A gallon of Bronner's costs $34.50 and can be used to wash floors, counters, dishes, and clothes. Like it says on the bottle, it's an "18 in 1 product." If you plan it right, you can fill a five-gallon pale with the right mixture of soap to water, and use it to wash all your dishes, clean your rig and then use the rest to wash your clothes. Planning is the key to making the most of your time and money on the road.

Washing Yourself

After I ditched deodorant, shampoo, and soap, my bathing/washing increased from every other day to two to three times a day. At first, I was an oily mess. My body had been producing more oil from the regular stripping and dehydrating that is caused by hard water and detergents.

This all normalized after about two weeks, and my skin got extremely soft to the touch. My hair looked like I spent hours putting product in it, when in fact I just let it do its thing. If I found myself oilier than normal, I played in some dirt. It would soak up the excess oil and rinse right off. We can debate the benefits of dirt/mud bathes later.

Be resourceful and utilize nature

Rivers, creeks, streams, and lakes make it very easy to rinse when needed. I understand that not having a conventional shower isn't for everyone. If you need to have one occasionally, try to plan it on a washing day. I'm ok with my natural body smell, but if you're not comfortable with yours, there are many natural deodorants you can make from natural ingredients that you have laying around and don't incur an additional cost.

WATER

THE AVERAGE SIZE TANK in a rig is about 25 gallons. Rationing and limiting water was the biggest adjustment I had to make from home life to bus life. If you want to get a feel for what this is like, fill up five 5-gallon buckets, turn off the water at home, and see how long that lasts you.

My rig only had a 10-gallon tank in it. Because I'm a backpacker I have a water filtration kit. I always had it in my hiking/go bag. Rather than bringing water with me, I would stop and fill a container while I was out. When it was wash day, I would bring a 5-gallon pail with me to fill and use. Between wash days, I would use a spray bottle filled with soap water and bottle filled with clean water to wash and rinse dishes. This method can also be used to wash counters, floors, and yourself if need be. Make sure to use the mist setting rather than the stream setting on the spray bottles to optimize water consumption.

Dogs are dogs and are going to drink from whatever water source they find. I always carried an empty gallon jug with me and would use that for his drinking water rather than the potable water.

Remember that when cooking, you're going to boil the water anyway, so why not use river water. I get that water is free, but to fill the tank requires driving, and driving requires gas, and that requires money.

Pay attention! Look everywhere for a water spigot. Even if your tank is only a gallon or two low, fill it.

You'd be surprised at how long you can make that extra gallon or two last. Allow time for needed resource restocking.

Take one trip for many
items instead of many
trips for single items.

FOOD

MOST OF WHAT I ATE and had for food was dried, canned, or vacuum packed. Canned food is cheap and lasts just about forever. Just the other day I made some chili from left over cans of beans, veggies, and canned meat from 2017.

We all know from experiences with Costco or Sam's club that buying in bulk leads to cheaper individual pricing. But this can get tricky with the limited space of living out of a vehicle. This is the reason why I only had a one cubic foot refrigerator in my bus. Not only did it free up space for more dry-can storage, but it limited my ability to have fresh food that can go bad. We all do it, put things in the fridge to get to later, only for it to go bad because of all the other food that goes in there to have later, and it gets forgotten. Having such a small space for perishables allows me to only buy for today.

> Learn to be ok with having fresh food only when it's close by.

No wasting fuel to go get lettuce for that sammy, looks like it's just meat and bread today.

Learn to Make It

Speaking of bread, yup that's right; don't buy any. Make your own. A loaf of whole wheat made at home comes out to about seventy-three cents per loaf. What's the actual cost? Seventy-three cents and three hours of your time, but that's why we're out here living this life, to do more things with our time, to experience more. There are some things that are just cheaper to buy, because of the process used to make those things. However, in general make everything you can. Buy as little prepared food as possible. If you don't meal plan already, I suggest you learn. One recipe might call for half a can of this and half a can of that, which means you are going to have to figure out what to make the next day to use both those half cans. Sometimes this means that your evening meal will consist solely of ½ a can of beans and ½ a can of tuna.

I told everyone I knew, that if they went out for food to not throw away their unused condiment packets. To this day I still have a bag of mixed variety single use condiments floating around.

The current prices are:

- 32 oz ketchup: $15.29

- 20 oz yellow mustard: $2.18

- 15 oz mayonnaise: $13.35

- 18 oz BBQ sauce: $3.48

- 36 oz ranch dressing: $5.47

Just to have the staples that are in everyone's fridge comes out to $39.77. We all know that one of those bottles in the fridge is bad. Let's add up the refrigerator space for all that.

103 oz is over 185 cubic inches! And that is if you put it all in one container. We all know that those containers take up an obscene amount of space and are not the least bit stackable. On the other hand, a paper bag full of single use condiments allows for tight storage and no refrigeration.

One of the practices I developed on the road and have stuck with to this day is based around my meat consumption habits. It started out as a way to save money when purchasing meat, and later it led to the realization that it was actually helping to mitigate the waste problem of factory farming meat. I only buy meat that is about to go bad. Like the managers special 75% off and it-needs-to-be-cooked-today about to go bad. I can buy a $20 steak for $5 and keep part of an animal's life from literally going in the garbage. This practice also means that you no longer go to the grocery store to pick up a hamburger, ribs, rack of lamb, bacon, or anything. You go to the grocery store to get protein in whatever form it presents itself that day. Remember were not running to the store everyday (unless you can walk or ride to it), so there is some planning involved.

I would always try to get things that were at least three days from the sell by date, allowing for a day to freeze and a day to defrost, and leaving one day grace period to getting around to cooking it. If it's something you plan on repackaging to allow for one meal preparation, remember to write on the new package how many days it had left before the sell by date.

Always ask for a manager when they will be doing the mark down foods. If there are five of

one item, offer to buy all of them if they will mark
it down even more. While I am writing this, it is
March 2022. Yesterday, I got sixty dollars of spe-
cialty dried salami and gourmet cheeses for ten
bucks, all because it cleared out shelf space for the
expensive stuff.

Make a lot of stew, soup, and do a lot of slow cooking

My protein cooking habits have also changed
to include this practice. Most of the tender good
to eat proteins get bought before hitting that sell
by date. It's usually the proteins that take a little
preparation that don't get bought before reaching
that date. Being left with the long process proteins
worked in my favor. It would leave more time to
come upon those fresh ingredients that I didn't
have but would add so much to the meal. It also
makes room for more appreciation while eating. In
the end, making all those meals are just all around
better and more connected.

Alternative Food Sources

Now to the questionable food sourcing. Food banks are meant to help those in need in the community. We are travelers trying to see as much of this country as we can and make our money stretch as far as we can. Does that put us in the "in need" category? For me it never did. Had I run completely out of money and had no other way to feed myself, I would have been able to use this resource. Talking to many food bank organizers about this over the years, never once was I met with, "This situation does not qualify you as in need of our services." It was always a gray area where everyone still felt comfortable helping alternate lifestyle individual such as us.

The other highly questionable acquisition of a free meal is walking into a hotel that offers free breakfast and coffee. This is considered stealing and therefore illegal; is it a punishable crime? Maybe that depends on the judge. I've known humans that do this, and that is why I'm including it. Again, I will not condone this action, but feel inclined to make note of it.

If you choose to go out for drinks, be sure to entertain your bartender. It can lead to discounted and even free drinks. You can even make bets for free drinks. I have the talent to be able to do handstands on bar stools. Yeah, I know; it's pretty unbelievable. All the bartenders I would tell this to were almost certain I was full of shit.

"You don't believe me, do you?"
"No, I really don't."
"I'm serious. I can fully press into one"
"Bull shit!"
"Ok. I'll bet you a night of drinks that I can."
"Sure. Why not?"

This has worked for me a handful of times. Simply entertaining them on a slow night can get you half-off drinks. This often requires some fenagling, but if you want to go for the blunt approach, this works just fine.

"It's fucking dead in here. You must be bored out of your mind. How 'bout I entertain you till it picks up and you feed me drinks?"

Trash Talk

Now to the nitty gritty. Dumpster diving. I've done this with other road lifers, but never out of necessity. Truly good food gets thrown away every day because of health and safety guidelines of the FDA. Restaurants that offer a replicated menu (doughnuts, bread, pastries, etc.) cycle out batches on a very regimented routine. It's as easy as walking in and asking an employee when the turnover time is for old to fresh product. You will know exactly when the good food will be found in the trash. Grocery stores do produce sweeps on a regular basis. This too can usually be found out simply by asking. Fast-food places toss any leftovers at the end of the night.

I once ran in to a rubber tramp that had a whole bunch of bar codes on the back of their phone. It took me a while to piece together the parts to this con, but when I did it made total sense and was genius. After I had put it all together, I asked them about it one day. I was right. They would go into a store and find an item that had a department mark down price. They would purchase said item, carefully remove the mark down sticker, and put it on the back of their phone. Then, any time they wanted they could go to that department and grab any item they wanted. Head to the self-checkout line and simply put the item on top of their phone and scan the discounted price. This was the most important part, it had to be for the department, not the individual item. When scanning, if the item in hand was different from the scanned item, it was easier to get caught. Again, this is one of those against the law things, but I'm committed to sharing every bit of information I gathered out there on the road.

Packaged foods require more handling and thus costs more. If you're in the PNW there is a wonderful store called Winco. The bulk foods section of this place is unbelievable. There are over 200 items ranging from cereal, trail mix, pancake mix, tea, candy, dried fruit, and gravy just to name a few. Try your best to shop the bulk foods section as much as possible. Remember, even the bulk foods have its dirt cheap, normal, and expensive varieties of foods. They always have at least six kinds of granola starting a $1 per pound all the way up to $7 per pound. Don't accidentally get the expensive version of the product. Also, don't get the cheap version and accidentally write down the expensive product code cause you looked up and slightly more to the right. Nothing is worse than paying for the wrong thing.

All the convenience stores that offer hot food or fresh daily food have guidelines for how long those foods can stay out. A safe bet is that at 10:00 pm they will clear everything for the day. Sometimes you can get it all for free. Sometimes you'll have to buy it because they can't technically give it away. But if you play it right, one dollar can buy the whole lot. This holds true at all-you-can-eat joints. What I would do is go in exactly five minutes before they close with a bunch of containers. I'd ask for the manager, give a brief run down that I'm trying to stretch money as far as I can, and I'd offer $5 to run through and grab what they are just going to throw away anyway. I would end up with food for a week from one run.

FUEL AND GO

I GUESS WE SHOULD TALK FUEL NOW. I used an app to check gas prices in the area. If I was taking a big trip, I would take an hour to plot my course and then check prices along the way, planning fuel stops so I always filled at the lowest price possible. Sometimes this means only putting in five gallons at one stop to make it to the other station where fuel is eighty cents cheaper. You must really know your route and rig to make this work. What mileage does your rig get at what speed? How well does it do in the mountains? Just how accurate is your tank gauge? Knowing this can save you. With a 100-gallon tank, saving 80 cents per gallon saves you $80. If it's a three-tank trip, that's $240 saved that trip. Say the lowest price was $3.20 a gallon, and you found that price for every fill, that trip would cost $960. But if you didn't plan it out and improvised and bought fuel at the highest price, that same trip could cost $1200.

Another consideration is determining the affect that the angle of incline/decline has on the suction of the fuel pump. What pump do you have? Is it electric in tank, or mechanical in engine? How clean is your tank? I've clogged more filters than I care to admit because of low fuel levels and sloshing. Diesel fuel collects moisture that can grow microbes, like mold, bacteria, and fungus (referred to as algae). You can be driving along smoothly one second and in an instant the engine chokes out and won't start. Or you can run smooth yesterday, and then today you can only do 35 mph before it starts to sputter. My bus has three filters; the algae is more like a slimy sludge that can in fact get all the way to the pump if its mechanical (which mine is). I actually prefer a mechanical pump. There are three bolts: pull the old one; put new one in, tighten bolts, boom you're done. That is of course assuming it's easy to get to the pump. My first bus required the removal of three other large items to get to the pump, but I digress.

Back to algae and filters. The mechanical pumps at inlet have a wire mesh screen as a last measure to keep particles out of the engine. Filter kits run around $160 to $250. Proper maintenance of fuel tank can significantly extend the time between replacement.

The last time I clogged my filters due to algae, I was headed back to Oregon from Middle of Nowheresville. I pulled into a fill station, topped off the tank and slept in the lot for the night. It was a cold fall morning, and I was on winding backroad driving a 40-foot Bluebird weighing in at 35,000 pounds. I couldn't go faster than 25 mph for about an hour, putting us far from civilization. Finally, we made it to a straight away and got to 35mph when jerk, jerk,

jerk. The engine sputtered and shut off. *FUCK!* I thought we blew the engine because it would not start; like it would not *at all*. Eventually, I determined it was a fuel issue and manually primed the lines, causing it to fire up. Luckily, I remembered seeing one of those old-time mechanic shops on a corner about ten minutes back. So, I limped the bus in, and we pulled filters. Yup, they were all clogged. It took about two hours for the new ones to get there; we got them in, fired it up, and I started down the road. But she still stalled out at 35 mph. Thankfully this mechanic had worked on diesels and said there's one more place to check. He pulled the mechanical pump and sure enough the metal filter was rusted; it was almost closed and clogged with algae. He pulled it out put the pump back in and we were golden. This cost me $900, and it would have cost around $2000, but the mechanic took care of it on his lunch break and didn't do it at the shop. That's right! This kind man worked on my bus on the side of the road over his lunch break.

Take Preemptive measures. Additives are a life saver.

Always put a little fuel dryer in after every fill. Always keep a filter kit or two on hand. Drop your tank the day you get it home and clean it out. Know your fuel lines; are they rubber or metal? How do they look? Keep a patch kit on hand: one for small leaks, one for big failures. Learn to get your rig to at least limp back to town and get it fixed. Do the research before hitting the road so you won't have to pay to have it fixed. And yes, I've blown fuel lines and had to fix them in a parking lot of a park before. It was not fun, and I got covered from head to toe in diesel fuel. However, it only cost $200 for the replacement lines, because thankfully it was all rubber hose.

Other Fuel Tips and Tricks

Truckers pay what's called PUC price, requiring them to only pay federal road taxes. It is calculated by each load and miles driven. Resulting in the price at the pump being significantly cheaper. Now,

I'm not saying to do this. In fact, I'm certain its actually illegal to do for noncommercial vehicles, but I do know some bus owners that will convince a trucker to run there PUC card and fill their bus at this extremely low price. I have also heard of some truckers that work for giant corporations, using the company fuel card to partially fill other rigs. Again, this is illegal, but I know it happens.

The legal way of doing this is what's called jugging. This is where you sit at a fuel station with and old school round metal fuel jug (because they look smaller than a new five-gallon jug; they are in fact the same size) and fly a sign all day until enough people are willing to fill the jug for a full tank. This is what I call desperate measures but is always an option. I've never had to do it, but I see it just about every time I pull into a station. You can either give the station a heads up that you're doing this, or risk getting the cops called on you.

Another extremely *legal* way to cut fuel prices is to own every fuel saver loyalty card there is. On top of the eighty cents, you could save from proper planning, loyalty cards can get you up to a dollar per gallon off at the pump. It's a hassle to keep track of all of it, but we live in a world of spread sheets on our phones, so it's actually kind of easy once you get it all logged.

If you have an air-top heater, hopefully you went with the diesel one. I know they are made to run off the vehicles fuel. So, if you don't have a diesel vehicle you obviously have to go with a gasoline air-top heater. But here's the trick. Always opt for the diesel heater. ALWAYS. Never hook it up to the vehicles tank. Instead add an auxiliary tank. There is a diesel option called off road, its dyed red and it has no road tax added to it. It's illegal to run a vehicle on it, but you can use it in tractors, for fuel oil, and recreational use. The last time I filled up my 25-gallon auxiliary tank for the heater, I ended up saving 20 bucks.

WHERE TO PARK

THE ENTIRE TIME I WAS ON THE ROAD, I never once stayed at a campground or an RV park.

Never pay for parking.

There are so many other options than paying $30 to park for a night. Most of the time, my focus on the road was climbing, so I parked in national forests, on BLM land, on grasslands, or in the middle of nowhere on a gravel pull out.

When not climbing and finding myself in society, parking was a bit tricky. I found that the best street parking was always next to a church, park, trail head, or dead-end street with open field at the end. These places always seemed to draw the least attention and allowed for longer term parking. All these options come with their own restrictions.

National Forests have a general parking limit of fourteen nights in one spot over the period of thirty days. Every fourteen nights, you need to move to a new site. It's best to put at least five miles between your new spot and the old one. One secret I learned from a forest ranger in the black hills, is that any of the pull offs with the informational signs are also deemed as a "site," meaning you can park here for up to fourteen nights. Which is what I did while climbing around the back side of Rushmore.

Now, if you get yourself way, way out there and haven't seen another human for ten days, that's ten days no one has seen you parked at that site. Which leads to that idyllic question, "If a tree falls in the forest, and no one is around to hear it, does it make a sound?"

Different forests will all have their own set of restrictions to the general rule of thumb. All designated sites will have the rules and regulations posted for that particular spot. There is approximately 193 million acres of land managed by the National Forest Service, so make sure to find out if that specific national forest has any limiting factors to *campability*. Generally, the more popular parks have monthly or yearly camping limits.

BLM (Bureau of Land Management) regulations are straight forward. You can park in one spot for fourteen days straight. This means you can park on one side of the road for fourteen days, then move to the other side for fourteen more days. Then you must move to a new location outside of a 25-mile radius of the previous location until the 29th day since the initial occupation. This is my favorite land service to use for long term parking. There's not much to do on BLM except wander in peace. As a result, they aren't big attractions for other humans and very quiet.

Like the National Forest, each area of the BLM will have separate governing restrictions in place for camping. You will find designated campsites, but the majority is park wherever and enjoy yourself. As long as there is not a "No camping" sign, you're good to go.

There are many hidden parking spots in the middle of nowhere.

My google maps is riddled with starred places I would find by just going to satellite mode and looking around. There are also a few apps out there that have a collection of places other humans have found along their travels. If you aren't already on the road, I suggest you start accumulating a map of parking spots around on the way to your destinations. Remember that dead-end roads make for amazing spots; just always make sure there is a turn around. Backing down a road for half a mile is doable but not fun.

Parking in town is tricky to say the least. Many have ordinances against sleeping in your vehicle in public parking spots. Some of these places will ticket if they catch you sleeping in your vehicle. I've gotten the knock several times. The thing I've learned is that if you answer they have absolute proof that you were in the vehicle during "night hours," and they can give you a ticket. If you don't answer and they can't see you inside the vehicle, they have no proof as to whether the vehicle was occupied. If they claim to have seen the vehicle moving, the simple answer is that was my dog. Remember that police need official complaints from private parking lots to have jurisdiction in said lot. They need proof that you are not allowed to be there to enforce any laws. The question, "Did you receive a complaint from the landowner?" is enough to shut their involvement down. This may sound aggressive, but when I was on the road, #vanlife wasn't a thing. I was regularly looked at as a potential problem. It's a completely different story now.

Anytime I tell anyone that I live out of a bus, eyes gloss over and they get those dreamy looks on their faces. I find it very ironic how idealized my lost, impoverished lifestyle is perceived these days. I mean think about it, I lived off $14,000 for four years. That's

$3,500 a year, $67.30 a week. Pan handlers make more than that in a day. Financially speaking, I was worse off than someone being homeless. I mean maybe that's why you're reading this now; maybe you have romanticized road life from a social media perspective. Now that it's been gentrified into a lifestyle choice for the elite, it's even more prominent.

Things have changed, and street parking is a little easier these days then when I was on the road. No one is really going to bother you for a night or even two in the same spot. The best bet for semi-long-term is still parking next to a church, park, trail head, or dead-end street with open field at the end. As churches are all about helping humans, neighbors don't really bother the happenings around a church. I do recommend a brief introduction to the head of the religious establishment to get the most out of your time there.

If choosing to stay around a park, high profile properties are not your best bet. You're going to have to find a smaller less traveled one to skirt under the radar.

Trail heads are usually open 24 hours and so is the parking at them. Now they are strictly for overnight parking, try not to hang out any longer than you need to, and you can get away with a good week of returning before really being noticed.

Dead-end streets are only going to be traveled by the residents of that street, so maybe say hi to some of them, and your parking should be slack.

Another example of the value of talking to everyone you meet. When I would be in town exploring and chatting, I would meet someone that was willing to let me park in their driveway, or they would know someone that had space for me. Like I said before, everybody knows somebody, and often you'll find someone that knows someone at your next location. Networking while on the road will always be your most helpful resource.

KEEP OPTIONS OPEN

WHEN I FIRST GOT ON THE ROAD, I kept a dual sport in the back of my bus, and I used that to make short runs. I would centrally park my bus so that I could get back and forth on one tank of gas on the bike.

Have an alternate mode of transportation

These days, electric motorcycles are relatively inexpensive and get up to 163 miles per charge. Since we run off solar, there is no cost to for electricity. With this option there is just the upfront cost and a minimal maintenance cost. The batteries are small enough to always keep an extra on hand. This gives you the ability to explore up to 163 miles away from base of operations.

For example, Alaska is the roundest state in the US. The square mileage of Alaska is 663,300. If you remember from geometry class, the equation for the area of a circle is $A = \varpi r^2$. With two batteries, you get a radius of 163 miles, giving you an area coverage of 83,468 miles from base camp.

$663300 \div 83468 = 7.9465803$

For this example, that is approximately eight basecamps. With basecamps being 326 miles apart giving you a total distance of 2282 miles to get from the first basecamp to the last. My bus gets twelve mpg at 60 mph.

$2282 \div 12 = 190$ gallons.

The average price per gallon of $3.20 x190 = $608. For $608 dollars you could explore the entire state of Alaska.

LIFE HACKS

DO YOUR RESEARCH for the major grocery stores in every region and get the loyalty cards. Get those points, and cash in on the savings.

*Never Ever Buy Anything
from a Convenience Store*

The reason is built right into the name convenience; roughly translated, it means inflated price. Also stay away from the impulse isles. Go into the store with a list and only get what's on the list. Your stomach will lie to you about what you actually need.

Here's my biggest hack:

`Make print outs of those barcodes`

Give them to the cashier and ask them to scan it anytime anyone doesn't use their loyalty card. The points you can rack up in a single day are insane. The one place this really killed was at 7-Eleven. Anywhere you go, you can always find one, and the points can be used to buy just about anything in the store, including warm meals.

Some grocery stores also have fuel stations and points can be used for money off price per gallon.

I've never once paid to get into a national park. Of the 419 national parks, only 119 have entrance fees. The ones that do are all the well-known, must-see parks. There are annual passes, pay by the vehicle, and per person fees ranging from $5 to $70. But if you understand the system, there is one big loophole. Are you ready for it? Ok here it is; it's the per vehicle fee. Here's what you do. Park your rig outside of the park and walk to the entrance. Look for a vehicle in line with an empty seat. Then use your charming communication skills to secure that empty seat. Ride through the entrance with them. Once across that imaginary entrance line, exit the vehicle and have a wonderful free day to yourself at that national park. Pretty underwhelming, isn't it? Let's do the math at a median of $30 per park.

$30 x 119 = $3,570 in savings.

That's a lot in terms of road life money.

Things You Don't Have to Pay For and Where to Get Them

- Ice: Almost every motel out there still has ice machines. Most gas stations or fast-food joints will let you fill up a Nalgene or two with ice if you just ask.

- Storage bags: You can find these in the bulk food section of the grocery store. They literally insist on giving these to you for your items. The large and medium bags require twist ties, but the small ones for the seasonings are usually the zip sealing types. You know it never hurts to double bag your items for safety.

- Just about anything: The dumpster is a good will sorting station. If you have the time and patience, you can find just about anything you might ever need. Good will has a store-to-store rotation routine, and once things have cycled through, more often than not it gets put in the dumpster.

- Coffee and soda: If you choose to be a bit shifty you can drink from any fast-food restaurant free. If you never throw away your cups, you can walk in and getting a refill.

Pay Attention

Pay attention when driving down backroads. Scan the fields and ditches around you. Learn what all the fruit trees look like. Learn to spot wild asparagus and other vegetables. Take the time to forage for food out on hikes. There are over 300 edible plants and fruits to forage. Remember the only cost here is some time and maybe a scratch or two from nature.

INSPIRE OTHERS

Tell your story.
Be happy.
Inspire others.
Put out good vibes to
the universe.

EVERY TIME I WOULD SHARE what I was doing, like actually share the why, the how, and how it was changing my life, whoever I was sharing it with would want to contribute in some way. Sometimes that meant I would get a meal bought to me. Usually, it was getting a name and a number of someone that could help at some point. One time, it meant getting a 1995 Geo Tracker valued at $1100 for $400. I even got a lot of climbing gear bought for me. When I was living at Miguel's Pizza in RRG, it often meant end of the night food, rides to town, invites to trips, beer, and often employees would tell other climbers that were flying home to leave any extra supplies with me.

Most importantly, give back all this generosity bestowed upon you by the universe.

That's why I do my best, since starting up DirtbagInnovations to make it affordable for other dirtbags, wanderers, wanderlust souls, and those in seek for the self the universe wants them to be and to get out there.

My time on the road, allowed me to tap into this other side of me. The part I didn't know existed. It's the part of us that hasn't evolved out of our DNA yet. You've probably felt bits of it occasionally: on a short trip, driving around with no place to be and end up at that unexpected stop to look at that thing. It's our ability to adapt quickly to new surroundings, to see the landscape and intuitively know everything it has to offer. Living this life, I was able to feel the life force it provides, and experience all of it. This experience helped me to be able to know when we've gotten everything we can from a place and not deplete its reserves. It's the nomadic side of us that pulls at us to move, to be able to find home in everything and everywhere. The world is our home and this instinctual side of us can teach us to respect her, to help her, to move around and take care of her. This is why you feel this sense of belonging when you leave the city and go deep into the quiet forest. Cherish the peace you will find on the road. Nothing quite compares to it.

AFTERWORD

AT THE END OF THAT FOUR YEARS ON THE ROAD, I found myself back in the place where it all started. I had about 700 dollars to my name, the pandemic had just started, and I was doing the city living thing. City living requires a lot of moving around to stay under the radar. As luck would have it, I ran into a van builder that was looking for custom aluminum fabrication. In November 2020, I started up Dirtbag Innovations, began developing aluminum products, and selling them to local Van Upfitters. After a few months of working with these companies, I realized that most of them had never lived the lifestyle they were selling. That's when I decided to expand out into the conversion industry. My goal is to bring all the experience and understanding I gained living on the road for almost a decade now to you and your build. If you are thinking about starting a build or have one already in the works that you need some help with, check out our website and feel free to reach out at:

www.dirtbaginnovations.com

Don't forget to check follow our instagram
@dirtbaginnovations

ACKNOWLEDGMENTS

I AM GRATEFUL TO THE SOULS that helped me acquire the knowledge, strength, and dedication to publish this book. None of you, or me for that matter, knew it was what we were doing at the time. None of you knew that your love gave me the strength to continue on every time I wanted to stop, or that the time I spent with you would give me the foundation to do what I did.

Ouppy, for fifteen years you were always by my side. I didn't know it till the day you passed away all that you had taught me about love, compassion, forgiveness, happiness, loyalty, understanding and finding happiness in helping others. You gave me everything and are my everything. I will always cherish and live in all the moments we had together. You are the reason I found my community and myself in that community. Every time I dream about you, I always wake up happy, because I know that this is the closest I will get to having you back. With all my love I will never let you go. I love you so much.

I had no idea that the lost wandering I did over the last six years would turn into a guidebook for others to help mitigate any of the big disasters on the road. For this, I owe my most sincere gratitude to all of you.

I am also grateful for having the courage to find myself over those four years on the road. If it weren't for that broken human being fed up and being so confused about who they were, I wouldn't be the self-loving, fulfilling human I am today.

ABOUT THE AUTHOR

ANTHONY STARTED BUILDING BUSES for themself. That's what they do. Their life has given them experience to not only build out rigs to fit the lifestyle, but they have also lived that lifestyle and they know what it entails.

Anthony works on helping others live a life full of experiences so that they can be true to themselves.

instagram.com/dirtbaginnovations

More from Dirtbag Innovations